AF531153

WHAT HAPPENED TO JUDGE CRATER?

by

Gail B. Stewart

Illustrated by

Marcy Ramsey

CRESTWOOD HOUSE
NEW YORK

Maxwell Macmillan Canada
Toronto

Maxwell Macmillan International
New York Oxford Singapore Sydney

Library of Congress Cataloging-in-Publication Data
Stewart, Gail.

What happened to Judge Crater? / by Gail B. Stewart. — 1st ed.
p. cm. — (History's mysteries)
Includes bibliographical references and index.
Summary: Discusses the mysterious disappearance of a New York judge in 1930 and presents three possible solutions.
ISBN 0-89686-617-3
1. Crater, Joseph Force, b. 1889—Juvenile literature. 2. Judges—New York (N.Y.)—Biography—Juvenile literature. 3. Missing persons—New York (N.Y.)—Case studies—Juvenile literature. [1. Crater, Joseph Force, b. 1889. 2. Judges. 3. Missing persons.] I. Title. II. Series.
KF373.C68S74 1992
347.747'03534—dc20
[B] 91-16554
CIP
AC

Crestwood House
Macmillan Publishing Company
866 Third Avenue
New York, NY 10022

Maxwell Macmillan Canada, Inc.
1200 Eglinton Avenue East
Suite 200
Don Mills, Ontario M3C 3N1

Macmillan Publishing Company is part of the Maxwell Communication Group of Companies.

First edition

Printed in the United States of America

10 9 8 7 6 5 4 3 2 1

CONTENTS

The Case Opens 5
The Case File 11
- Who *Was* Judge Joseph Force Crater? 11
- "A Wild and Ruthless Time" 12
- The Seabury Investigation 15
- And Prohibition Too 16
- A Chance of a Lifetime 19
- A Supreme Court Justice 22
- Looking for Clues 22
- The Final Day? 24
- The Last Hours 26
- The Mysterious Drawer 28
- Goodtime Joe? 30
- A Crooked Judge? 31
- Too Many Questions, Not Enough Answers 32

Solutions 37
- Disappeared on Purpose 37
- Killed by Blackmailers 38
- Murdered for What He Knew 40

Closing the Case File 42
Chronology 45
Resources 46
Index 47

THE CASE OPENS

Stella Crater wasn't worried, but she *was* annoyed. It was Saturday, August 9, 1930, her 43rd birthday. She had expected to celebrate it with her husband, Joe, at their cabin in Maine, but he wasn't there.

Judge Joseph Force Crater had gone into New York City on business six days earlier. According to Stella's book, *The Empty Robe,* before the judge left, he told her he'd be back "probably either Wednesday or Thursday. But I'll surely be here before your birthday on Saturday."

Friends who owned cabins near the Craters' drove Stella into the little town of Belgrade Lakes. They met the incoming train on Thursday and then again on Friday. Joe was not on either train.

Stella was not concerned. Her husband was a

busy man. He was involved in politics in New York, and she understood that he worked hard. Often, time got away from him.

She was confident that Joe would be on the train from New York on Saturday. After all, he had promised not to miss her birthday. They planned to celebrate with two other couples. The six of them would play cards, eat ice cream and cake, and perhaps go for a moonlight swim in the lake.

But Joe was not on Saturday's train either.

Early in the afternoon, a truck pulled up to the Craters' cabin. It was Irv Bean, who ran a store in Belgrade Lakes. He brought a big new canoe. It was painted bright red. Bean told Stella that Joe had ordered it for her as a birthday gift. Since Joe was not back yet, Bean said, he thought he might as well bring it to the cabin.

Stella and her friends had the party without Joe. They all assumed he would be home in a day or two.

But Sunday and Monday passed without a sign from Joe. Stella was more than a little concerned now. Something had to be wrong, or Joe would have come. Was he sick? Had he been in an accident?

On Monday Stella could stand the waiting no longer. She walked two miles to the Sacketts' cabin since the Craters did not have a telephone in theirs.

She called Simon Rifkind, a lawyer who worked in the same office with Joe.

Rifkind was not alarmed. He reassured Stella that everything was probably fine. He told her he would ask around and get back to her. In the meantime, he said, she shouldn't worry.

But Stella did worry. It was not like Joe to disappear.

Several days after calling Simon Rifkind, Stella sent Fred Kahler, the Craters' chauffeur, to New York. She instructed him to go to their apartment, Joe's law office and anywhere else Fred could think to look.

A few days later, Stella received a note from Fred. He wrote that everything seemed to be all right. Although he hadn't seen the judge, Crater's business associates were not concerned. "Everybody says he had been around and is all right," wrote Fred.

Stella Crater wrote that she remembered that when Fred returned to Belgrade Lakes, he told her that Judge Crater's political friends had told him "not to hang around too much." They told Fred that it might cause newspaper reporters to be suspicious. If word leaked out that the judge was not around, it might make people think he was irresponsible. And, Fred was told, an irresponsible judge would certainly not win the next election!

Stella Crater was a little relieved that things "seemed to be okay," as Fred put it. She told herself her husband would turn up soon, and the "mystery" would be solved. After all, an important man like Joe Crater—a state Supreme Court justice—could not just vanish.

Then on August 25 Stella received an urgent telephone call. Justice Louis Valente, who worked with Joe, wanted to know why he had not come to work. The Supreme Court had started back to work that day after a summer break. Where was Joe?

There was no reassuring explanation for Joe's absence. He loved his work, and only a tragedy would cause him to miss a court date. Something was terribly wrong, Stella felt.

Stella returned to New York City. Trying to control her panic, she contacted anyone and everyone who knew Joe. Had they seen him? When was the last time? Had he said anything that might explain his disappearance?

No one knew anything. Stella had no choice but to call the police. She contacted the Missing Persons Bureau. They began work right away on case number 13595.

Within hours Judge Crater's disappearance had become news. The front page of every New York paper carried his picture and a story. Police roamed the city, looking for leads. Flyers appeared on every street corner, announcing that the city would pay $5,000 to anyone who could lead them to the judge.

And Stella Crater waited, hoping for news.

EXTRA!!
JUDGE VANISHES
NEWS STAND
EXTRA DAILY MIRROR EXTRA
JUDGE CRATER DISAPPEARS!
State Supreme Court
Judge MISSING!
BANK OF
DAILY
MIRR

THE CASE FILE

WHO *WAS* JUDGE JOSEPH FORCE CRATER?

Detectives working on missing persons cases have difficult jobs. They need to have a good idea about just who the missing person is. The background of a person almost always offers clues. Knowing as much as they can about a person's habits, character, friends and family helps detectives find likely places to search.

What kind of person was Judge Crater?

The kind who always knew what he wanted to be—a lawyer. He was born in 1889 in Pennsylvania. *Saturday Evening Post* reporter Jack Alexander learned from Crater's sister that as a young boy Joe dreamed of being a judge.

Crater graduated from Columbia Law School in New York City and set to work making a practice for himself. In 1916 he met a young woman named Stella Mance Wheeler when he handled her divorce. In 1917, just one week after the divorce became final, Joe and Stella were married.

Crater seemed bound for success. He was an excellent lawyer. He was also fascinated by politics—especially on the state level. As a young lawyer, he became involved in a club for Democrats on New York City's West Side. He put in long hours making speeches, attending meetings and learning how New York politics worked.

"A WILD AND RUTHLESS TIME"

There was a great deal to learn about power and politics in New York in the years between 1920 and 1930. Much of it was corrupt and dirty. Since the late 1800s, the Democratic party had controlled the political power in New York City. The power within the party was a group of politicians known as Tammany Hall. They were named that after the building in which they had their headquarters.

Many Tammany Hall politicians remained in office for a long time. They often won elections by illegal means. One such way was by taking

advantage of immigrants who came to New York in the late 19th century.

Most of the immigrants who settled in the city had arrived by boat from Europe. They arrived poor and hungry. Most spoke no English. Their chances of getting good jobs were slim.

The Tammany Hall politicians often promised them money, better housing and jobs. But such promises had a price. The immigrants were expected to "pay" with their votes. Sometimes the jobs and better housing didn't come through, but the immigrants were still expected to keep the politicians in office.

This kind of corruption was all over New York, in elected officials, police, lawyers and judges. If a person had enough money or connections, he could get away with almost anything. A businessman who operated a gambling house in New York, for instance, was taking a large risk of being jailed. However, if the businessman knew a judge or had the money to bribe police officers, he had almost nothing to fear.

Sometimes the public got angry about the corruption in their government. Occasionally, they called for reform and elected a mayor or other official who promised to clean up New York politics.

But such reformers did not last long. Because they did not offer bribes to police or judges, they received no support from the rest of the government. These reformers usually served only one term before Tammany Hall forced them out of office. In fact, the corrupt political system was so efficient it was sometimes called the Tammany Machine.

THE SEABURY INVESTIGATION

In fact, at the time of Judge Crater's disappearance, there was a large investigation of Tammany Hall underway. Samuel Seabury had orders from the state legislature to find out just how far the corruption in New York had spread.

Seabury was a former member of the New York Supreme Court. He had seen evidence of payoffs and bribery many times as a judge. He was determined to find out who was dirty and who was clean.

What the Seabury Commission found was no real surprise. Rich people usually received special favors from the city. After just six months of careful investigation, Seabury and his staff had investigated the activities of 2,260 people.

In February 1932 an article about Seabury appeared in the *Literary Digest.* In the article Seabury was portrayed as "swinging a mighty brush dipped in printer's ink." Seabury was, according to the reporter, "painting fresh stripes of deepest black on the Tammany Tiger."

Seabury did succeed in "painting the Tammany Tiger"—showing the extent of the city's problems. One of the most troublesome of these problems was the bribing of officials by criminals and others in exchange for favors.

Seabury found dozens of city, state and county employees who were mysteriously depositing huge sums of money in personal bank accounts. The sheriff of New York County, for instance, had a bank balance that jumped to almost $400,000 in six years—on an annual salary of $18,500!

It was, according to the *Washington Post* in 1932, a "strangle grip which the Tammany Tiger holds on New York's throat."

AND PROHIBITION TOO

The corruption of Tammany Hall was bad. But during the years Joe Crater was beginning his career, there were even worse problems. The years between 1920 and 1933 were the years of Prohibition, when it was illegal to make, sell or use alcoholic beverages in the United States. Prohibition began in 1920 when the Congress of the United States passed a special amendment to the Constitution.

Not everyone was willing to give up alcohol. In fact, there was such demand for liquor during Prohibition that illegally selling it, or bootlegging, became a big business.

In cities like New York and Chicago secret drinking clubs called speakeasies opened. Because the clubs were illegal, the owners needed protection from the law in order to exist. In New York Tammany Hall operated several speakeasies. They even conducted important political meetings in them.

In *The End of the Roaring Twenties* Bill Severn wrote, "Everybody knew that bootleg syndicates and speakeasies couldn't operate without putting police, sheriffs and other officials on their payrolls. There was hardly any state, county or large city where charges were not brought at one time or another that officials were working with the liquor gangs."

Not all New York politicians and police were criminals. But as young Joe Crater became more

and more involved in New York politics, he could not help noticing the corruption of Tammany Hall.

What did Crater learn from the corruption around him? Opinions differ. His wife later wrote that "there was not a more honest man alive than Joe." She could not believe that Judge Crater could have become as dirty as the political system around him.

But others, like writer Murray Teigh Bloom, disagreed. Bloom thought Crater learned and used every bit of what the Tammany Hall leaders taught him. "If he'd been straight, he could have gone far," Bloom said in a 1960 *New York Times* article, "but he was crooked."

A CHANCE OF A LIFETIME

In 1920 Crater began working for Judge Robert F. Wagner. Wagner was a leading Tammany official and a justice of the New York Supreme Court. He needed a sharp young law clerk, and Joe Crater filled the bill.

Crater was a great success at his job. Much of the work was dull, but Crater did not mind. He was aware that good lawyers had to spend many hours in file rooms of police stations and law libraries. "He had not balked at performing any of the sweatier chores that came his way," wrote Jack Alexander in a 1960 *Saturday Evening Post* article. Crater showed himself to be a thorough, careful worker.

Judge Wagner appreciated Crater's abilities too. He gradually gave him more and more responsibilities. Soon Crater was a constant companion to the judge. In her book Stella Crater remembers her husband once bragging that Wagner "wouldn't buy a hat without me to advise him."

Crater was ambitious—he had goals that he wanted to achieve. Yet those who knew him said that he knew how to wait. Crater was smart enough to put his ambition on the back burner. His most important task while working for Judge Wagner's large law offices, he said, was to learn.

"Wagner is an important man in the party," Joe once told his wife. "If I do well . . . it is certain to bring me to Wagner's attention. And you have to have the right kind of people behind you to get anywhere in politics."

In 1927 Judge Wagner was elected to the U.S. Senate. Crater decided to go into private practice. He had worked for Wagner for seven years. It was time, he told his wife, that he make it on his own.

A SUPREME COURT JUSTICE

Early in 1930 a New York Supreme Court justice named Joseph Proskauer resigned. There were still several months left in his term.

Franklin D. Roosevelt was then governor of New York and he offered the post to Joe Crater. Crater was sworn in on April 8, 1930. In her book *The Empty Robe* Stella remembers feeling hurt and resentful that she was left out of Joe's decision. She had no idea that such a position might be offered to him. She was not even present during his swearing-in ceremony.

Joe told her he preferred to keep her separate from his political life. "There's a lot of political maneuvering which you simply wouldn't understand," he told her. The new job would be good for his career, he reminded her. "It carries an annual salary of $22,500. And listen to this," he confided to her, "no less than F. D. R. himself has said that I have it in me to go all the way to the United States Supreme Court!"

LOOKING FOR CLUES

In April 1930 Joe Crater seemed to be a rising star in New York politics. Yet just four months later he vanished, apparently without a clue. What had happened?

Police did a thorough search of his apartment. Stella Crater carefully looked through her husband's closet. She found a brown-and-green pinstriped suit missing. His suitcases were all in his closet, and nothing else appeared to be gone.

What wasn't missing, however, puzzled the detectives. The judge's pocket watch and chain and his best fountain pen were on the dresser. Judge Crater never went out without these things, according to his wife. They were special to him, for they carried his initials, she told police.

Detectives next tried to figure out the judge's whereabouts on the day he came back to New York from Belgrade Lakes. Had he ever arrived in the city? And if so, when was the last time he had been seen?

They learned that Judge Crater had indeed arrived safely in New York from Maine. He had spoken to his maid on Monday, August 4. The following day he had lunch with a fellow judge. That night, he had dined with a doctor friend.

The doctor remembered that Crater had gone home about midnight. The Craters' maid said that when she came to work on the sixth, she found the bedclothes mussed. The judge had undoubtedly slept in his own bed that night.

THE FINAL DAY?

August 6 was the last day anyone remembered seeing the judge. Joe Crater worked in his office the day he disappeared. One of the lawyers who sometimes worked with Crater reported that he saw the judge reading certain folders. The lawyer said that Crater was pulling papers out of files. He was stashing them in two leather briefcases and five cardboard portfolios.

That morning, Judge Crater called Joseph Mara, his court attendant, into his office. He gave Mara two checks totaling $5,150. The checks were made out to cash. Crater asked Mara to cash them.

When Mara came back with the cash and handed it to Crater, the judge did not even count the money. He put the two envelopes into the inside pocket of his suit jacket. Mara said that after he gave the judge the money, Crater locked himself in his office and stayed there for almost two hours.

A little after noon, Crater called Mara into his office again. Crater showed him five large portfolios filled with papers. He wanted them fit into two briefcases.

Mara packaged the papers as Crater asked. Crater asked his secretary to lock up the office, and he and Mara left with the heavy briefcases. Mara told detectives that he and Crater took a cab to Crater's apartment. He carried the briefcases inside for the judge, put them on a chair in the living room, then left.

Mara insisted later that he had no idea what was in the briefcases. He was also unsure why the judge wanted the papers brought to his home.

THE LAST HOURS

No one the police talked to could explain what the judge did that afternoon. However, he was seen again that evening.

Joseph Grainsky ran the Arrow Theater Ticket Agency on Broadway. He remembered Judge Crater wanting a ticket for a comedy called *Dancing Partners*. Grainsky had no tickets at the time, but he told Crater to come back later and he'd try to get one. If Grainsky could find a ticket, he would leave it at the box office.

From the ticket agency Crater walked to Billy Haas's Restaurant on West 45th Street. It was about 8:00 P.M., and he hoped to eat and get to the theater by the 9:00 P.M. curtain time.

When Crater entered the restaurant, he heard his name being called. He looked around and saw a friend, William Klein. Klein was a lawyer who worked for theater people. Since the theater was something that interested Crater, he enjoyed talking with Klein.

There was a woman with Klein that night, a showgirl named Sally Lou Ritz. Both Klein and Ritz invited the judge to join them for dinner, and he gladly accepted.

Klein told police later that the judge seemed in excellent spirits. He was excited about seeing the play that evening. He also mentioned that he was going up to Maine for his wife's birthday.

The dinner went on past nine, recalled Klein. But Crater decided to catch what he could of the play. He left at the same time as Klein and Ritz. The three walked outside into the warm summer evening, talking and laughing.

Judge Crater hailed a taxi and got in. The tan-colored cab headed west on 45th Street. Klein and Ritz watched the cab for a moment, then began walking in the opposite direction down 45th.

That was the last any person was known to have seen Judge Joseph Force Crater.

THE MYSTERIOUS DRAWER

The police had searched the Craters' apartment. They had not found a note from Crater or any sign of the briefcases Mara had mentioned. So they were surprised when Stella Crater called them in January 1931. She had found envelopes in a secret dresser drawer. One of these envelopes, she said, contained a letter from her husband!

The police came and studied the envelopes. One contained $6,690 in cash, another held some bonds and stock certificates. A third enclosed insurance policies on Judge Crater's life totaling $30,000.

The fourth envelope was marked "Confidential—S. M. W."—Stella's initials. Inside was a handwritten letter. It listed the names of 20 companies or people who owed Crater money. In the letter Crater urged his wife to get in touch with them, for, as he wrote, "they will surely pay their debts." The note ended with the scrawl, "Am very weary. Love, Joe."

The police were boggled. They had checked all the drawers, even the "secret" drawer in September, and the envelopes had not been there. How had they gotten there in the time since then?

GOODTIME JOE?

A grand jury tried hard to solve the mystery of Judge Crater's disappearance. A grand jury decides whether there is enough evidence of a crime for a trial to be held or for further official investigation to be made. In the course of that investigation, a very different side of the judge was revealed.

It seemed as though Crater was leading a double life. One side was the thoughtful, loyal husband. The other side of Judge Crater was a dandy who was nicknamed Goodtime Joe by many women who knew him.

Detectives found, for instance, that Crater had visited the apartment of an attractive divorced woman on a regular basis. The woman worked as a salesperson and model in a local shop. Judge Crater paid a portion of the woman's rent. Crater was also on friendly terms with several showgirls. Police found witnesses who had often seen Crater escorting various women to New York nightclubs. Some of these women were known to have had connections with New York criminals.

One of the showgirls, June Brice, claimed that everyone liked the judge. He sometimes helped them out. Using his connections and influence, he helped them land roles in shows around town.

A CROOKED JUDGE?

The grand jury had shown that Judge Crater's personal life was a puzzle. The investigation also raised questions about his professional life.

For instance, Judge Crater had taken part in a business deal involving the bankrupt Libby Hotel in New York. There was a lot of talk that the deal was crooked, and that the judge had used his influence to help certain people make a lot of money. In fact, the Seabury Commission was interested in the facts of the case too.

In 1929 Judge Crater had acted as the receiver for the big hotel on the Lower East Side. As a receiver, Crater controlled the funds of the property and collected any monies due. He also was in charge of selling it when the finances had been cleared up.

The American Mortgage Loan Company bought the hotel in June 1929. The company had bid $75,000 for the building, and Crater approved the sale.

The suspicious part came two months later. The city was planning a street-widening project. The Libby Hotel was in the way, so the city had to condemn the property. The price the city paid for the hotel was $2,850,000. That worked to a profit of more than $2.7 million for the American Mortgage Loan Company.

There was a great deal of talk about the deal. Had Crater known about the street-widening project before he sold the hotel? Had he been bribed to sell it for the low price of $75,000?

The rumors grew, too, because the Libby Hotel was one of the names on the list Crater left for his wife. According to the note he wrote on the list, there was a very large sum of money due him "for service." What role had Judge Crater played in the Libby Hotel deal?

TOO MANY QUESTIONS, NOT ENOUGH ANSWERS

The grand jury investigation came up with more questions than answers. By the time they were through, the investigators had more than 975 pages of testimony. They had spent three months and thousands of dollars. However, they were still unable to discover how and why Judge Crater had disappeared.

Many felt that the evidence suggested the judge was dishonest. They pointed to the close ties he had had with Tammany leaders like Mayor Jimmy Walker and Judge Martin Healy, both accused of wrongdoing by the Seabury investigators.

Crater's corruption was hinted at even more strongly. Reports suggested that he might have paid for his seat on the New York State Supreme Court. New York newspapers reported that on May 27, 1930, Crater had sold stocks worth $15,779 and had withdrawn $7,500 from his personal bank account. The total amount was, according to the New York *World-Telegram,* "suspiciously close to the $22,500 annual salary of a Supreme Court Justice."

The article stated that investigators suspected that "Crater may have been abiding by the old ward heeler's rule of thumb—a year's salary for any political plum granted."

Those who believe strongly that Crater was dishonest were convinced that he might have been murdered. Was it to keep him from testifying about other Tammany leaders who were corrupt? Was he killed in a dispute about payoffs or bribes in a case like that of the Libby Hotel?

Others who have investigated the case feel he disappeared on purpose. They say that maybe he knew he was in danger from Tammany Hall because he knew too much. By taking a new identity and leaving town, he escaped with his life.

For a long time after Judge Crater's disappearance, the police were given tips by people who claimed to have seen him. According to such tips, Crater was prospecting in California, working as a lawyer in Maine or hitchhiking through Mexico. As one New York detective said, "You name the place and the judge has been seen there."

None of these leads ever proved valuable. However, the New York police were kept busy following up on them.

Judge Crater's family was hit hard by his disappearance. The rumors that he was involved in illegal activities hurt his wife and parents. His father died in 1940, a confused man who did not know whether he should be proud or ashamed of his son.

Crater's wife suffered ill health, but tried to clear his name. She remarried several years later, but the marriage failed. She told friends she was still hopelessly in love with Joe and always would be.

The judge's mother lived until 1951. Until her death she was convinced that her son was alive and that he would return someday. Each day, she and her daughter Margaret talked about Joe's disappearance, trying to make sense of it all.

"We would go into the matter every day," Margaret later told reporter Jack Alexander. "We

BROADWAY
BANK

would argue the pros and cons by the hours, until we realized that we were repeating ourselves. When she died, I was holding her hand. I remember that when she stopped breathing I said to myself, 'Now, at last, she knows.' "

You have just read the known facts about one of HISTORY'S MYSTERIES. To date, there have been no more answers to the mysteries posed in the story. There are possibilities, though. Read on and see which answer seems the most believable to you. How would you solve the case?

SOLUTIONS

DISAPPEARED ON PURPOSE

Judge Crater had a great deal to fear from the Seabury investigations. He had paid for his appointment to the State Supreme Court. He had broken laws in his handling of the Libby Hotel sale. Being charged with such crimes would bring humiliation and the end of his political career. He would also no longer be allowed to practice law.

Crater decided to disappear. He did not even tell his wife of his plans, although he did make arrangements for her finances. He went back to New York from his cabin in Maine on August 3. In his office he carefully went over all his files. He pulled out those that might show evidence of his crimes. These he later burned. He asked his assistant, Joseph Mara, to cash two checks totaling more than $5,000 to pay for his plan.

Crater disappeared on August 6 after eating a restaurant dinner. He bought a train ticket under a false name and went to California. He settled there for a time, then went to Mexico, where he lived until his death.

KILLED BY BLACKMAILERS

Judge Crater was friends with showgirl June Brice. He told her about his business dealings, including the Libby Hotel deal. Brice had connections with New York gangsters. She told them.

The gangsters decided to blackmail Crater. They visited him in the summer of 1930 to give him a choice—pay or they would go to the police with what they knew.

Crater was frightened. The truth would destroy his career. On the other hand it would be hard to get the cash the blackmailers wanted quickly.

The checks his assistant, Joseph Mara, cashed on August 6 were less than the blackmailers wanted. Crater had decided to tell the blackmailers that $5,000 was as much as he would pay.

A meeting was set up for that evening. The blackmailers picked Crater up in a cab at the restaurant. They drove to an abandoned ware-

TAXI

house. Crater told them to take $5,000 or he himself would go to the police. The gangsters shot Crater and dumped his body in the nearby Hudson River.

MURDERED FOR WHAT HE KNEW

Crater had worked for Judge Robert Wagner for years. Although Wagner was never accused of wrongdoing by the Seabury investigators, many of his associates were. Crater had met most of those associates. Crater himself tried to remain honest, but he knew a lot.

As the Seabury investigators looked deeply into Tammany corruption, the Tammany leaders grew frightened. They thought that Crater might testify against them. Some of them had criminal connections. They hired gangland killers to deal with Crater if he wouldn't listen to reason. He wouldn't.

He went to Maine, hoping the whole thing would blow over. It didn't. He received a telegram early in August, telling him to go back to New York. He went.

There he put his papers in order and arranged to get financial information to his wife. On August 6 he was forced into a car outside a New York theater. He was taken to a house outside of the city and killed. His body was dumped in the Hudson River.

CLOSING THE CASE FILE

The New York grand jury could not close the Crater case. There were too many questions. Witnesses were not always reliable. There were not enough hard facts to back up some of the stories about the judge. In the 1930s and after there was even a popular phrase—"to pull a Crater." That meant to disappear without fulfilling one's responsibilities.

Comedians of the time told Judge Crater jokes. People looking under a cushion or chair could say they were looking for Judge Crater and get a laugh.

But Crater's story did more than tickle people's funnybones. For years after his disappearance people called the New York police. Some said they had seen Crater. Others claimed to have talked with him. Some even said they had worked with him. Many stories were just that—stories. But there was always the chance that one of the stories was true. Police tried to keep an open mind and follow up leads that seemed possible.

People who weren't police officers worked on the Crater case too. Murray Teigh Bloom, a writer who had long been fascinated by the Crater case, visited Holland in 1955. He talked to a psychic named Gerard Croiset. Croiset had the reputation of being able to put himself into a trance and solve mysteries. Murray Bloom hoped Croiset could solve the Crater case.

Bloom showed Croiset a photograph of Judge Crater but didn't say who the man in the picture was. Bloom was certain that Croiset was unfamiliar with the case. After he had gone into a trance, Croiset said that the man in the picture had been murdered. He said that the murderer was a Chicago businessman, whom he called Mr. A.

Bloom became convinced that Crater had been murdered in Yonkers, a suburb near New York City. The case became more interesting when Bloom talked with a police officer who knew about a butcher named Henry Krauss.

Henry Krauss had once told the officer he owned a house in Yonkers. He sometimes lent the house to politician friends. Krauss claimed that Crater had been murdered in the house. His body was buried in the garden outside.

In 1960 *Life* magazine got permission from the house's new owners to dig in the garden. Croiset helped by trying to pinpoint the burial site. The digging turned up nothing.

An unsolved mystery is a challenge. Even if Judge Crater had not been murdered, it is doubtful he would be alive today. He would be over 100 years old. But people still study old documents and newspaper clippings, hoping to find overlooked clues. Perhaps someday someone will shed new light on Judge Crater and his strange disappearance. For now he remains hidden in the shadows.

CHRONOLOGY

1917	March 16, Joseph Crater marries Stella.
1920	June 15, Crater begins working for Justice Robert F. Wagner.
1927	Crater leaves Wagner's offices.
1929	February 2, Crater becomes receiver of Libby Hotel. June 27, Libby Hotel is sold to American Mortgage Loan Company. August 9, Libby Hotel is sold to New York City.
1930	April 8, Crater appointed to New York State Supreme Court. mid-April Seabury investigation begins. late June Crater joins Stella in Maine. early July First indictments of Seabury Commission. August 3, Crater leaves Maine for New York City. August 6, Crater disappears.
1931	January 9, Grand jury fails to resolve Crater case.
1960	November *Life* magazine unsuccessfully searches grounds of house in Yonkers for Crater's body.

RESOURCES

SOURCES

Baldwin, Hanson W., and Shepard Stone (eds.). *We Saw It Happen*. New York: Simon and Schuster, 1938.

Crater, Stella. *The Empty Robe*. Garden City, N.J.: Doubleday, 1961.

Myers, Gustavus. *The History of Tammany Hall*. New York: Dover, 1971.

Northrop, William B. *Insolence of Office*. New York: G. P. Putnam's Sons, 1931.

FURTHER READING FOR YOUNG READERS

Lindop, Edmund. *The Turbulent Thirties*. New York: Franklin Watts, 1970.

Severn, Bill. *The End of the Roaring Twenties*. New York: Messner, 1969.

INDEX

A., Mr., 43
American Mortgage Loan Company, 31, 32
Arrow Theater Ticket Agency, 26

Belgrade Lakes, Maine, 5–7, 23
Billy Haas's Restaurant, 26
Bloom, Murray Teigh, 19, 43
Brice, June, 30, 38

Croiset, Gerard, 43–44

Healy, Martin, 32

Kahler, Fred, 7–8
Klein, William, 27
Krauss, Henry, 43

Libby Hotel deal, 31–32, 33, 37

Mara, Richard, 24–26, 28, 37, 38

Prohibition, 16–17

Rifkind, Simon, 7
Ritz, Sally Lou, 27
Roosevelt, Franklin D., 22

Seabury Commission, 15, 32, 37, 40

Seabury, Samuel, 15–16
speakeasies, 17

Tammany Hall, 12–17, 19, 32–33, 40

Valente, Louis, 8

Wagner, Robert F., 19–20, 40
Walker, Jimmy, 32

Yonkers, New York, 43–44